AF413162

BE YOUR OWN PAL!

Copyright © 2023 by Duc Chung MD, MBA, FAAHPM

All rights reserved. No part of this book may be reproduced in any manner whatsoever without written permission except in the case of brief quotations embodied in critical articles and reviews.

First Printing, 2023

# Be Your Own PAL!

## Positive Affirmations
## for Life

DUC CHUNG MD, MBA, FAAHPM

Duc Chung MD, MBA, FAAHPM

# CONTENTS

# DEDICATION

*This book is dedicated to YOU. Here's to YOU.*

# "BE YOUR OWN PAL" JOURNEY

Thank you for the opportunity to share this *Positive Affirmations for Life (PAL)* journey with you. Many of us struggle with depression, anxiety, low self-worth, and doubt. We can be our own worst enemies. Positive affirmations can change that. Instead of enduring self-defeat, we can win in life by being our own *PALs*. We can learn to love ourselves truly, deeply, and unconditionally. Through this ten-day journey, you will positively influence your sense of self through awareness, compassion, gratitude, healing, and love. This is a journey of *self-discovery*. You are strong. You are worthy. You are your greatest asset for a bigger and better you.

# INTRODUCTION

Positive affirmations are positive phrases and statements that help challenge negative thoughts and emotions that are toxic to our physical and mental health. Affirmations can change lives.

There are three essential Ps for writing positive affirmations: Present tense, Positive, and Personal.

**Present tense**, instead of the future tense, actuates your vision. For example, if you struggle with low self-worth, a positive affirmation can be "I love myself each and every day" instead of "I will love myself each and every day." The present tense attracts the here and now and gives you a sense of truly living your affirmation.

**Positive** refers to what you want rather than what you do not want. For example, if you are being considered for a work promotion, you want to avoid negative affirmations such as "I am not good or worthy of that promotion." Instead, "I am good and more than worthy of that promotion" instills belief in success.

**Personal** refers to your actions and behaviors. You have full control over your own outcomes. For example, if you struggle with weight gain and low body image, a positive affirmation can be "I work out every day and I am looking my very best." Impersonal statements such as "That weight loss program will help me look better" make the future uncertain and ungratifying. Action is what matters.

There are many ways to practice positive affirmations. Some prefer to speak or read them out loud. Some prefer to record, listen, and visualize the affirmations coming to life. Some may only prefer to recite them silently. Whatever method is most suitable for you, set aside at least three to five minutes a day for deep reflection. It is best to repeat each affirmation at least ten times and write them fully on paper as you go. As you repeat your affirmations, take a few deep breaths and breathe them into life. *Let's get started.*

# DAY 1: AFFIRMATIONS FOR SELF-AWARENESS

*"Self-awareness is our capacity to stand apart from ourselves and examine our thinking, our motives, our history, our scripts, our actions, and our habits and tendencies."*
*~ Stephen Covey*

Welcome to your first day. Today, let's find a sacred space to reflect on who you are as a person without any judgment or criticism.

To begin, take five deep breaths to center yourself. As you do so, pick a positive affirmation that resonates with you below and recite it to yourself ten times. It is best to do this in a quiet space or in front of a mirror. Take five more deep breaths when you are finished.

- *I accept myself for who I am today.*
- *I am not perfect, but I am working on becoming better every day.*
- *I have the right to be who I want to be without judgment or criticism.*
- *I am not my past; I am the person I have become.*
- *I am not responsible for the past; I am responsible for the future.*
- *I am a bigger, better, and stronger person for all that I have been through.*
- *I am a person of value and worth, no matter what anyone says about me.*
- *I am someone who is always learning and improving my skills.*
- *I am a person of courage amidst adversity.*
- *I am a fearlessly resilient person.*

When you are ready, fill the following pages with your own self-awareness affirmations. Remember to be present, positive, and personal. *I am* and *I believe* statements along with positive verbs and adjectives are powerful. After you recite your own affirmations, take five more deep breaths and give yourself a nice, big hug. Repeat this exercise as many times as you find helpful.

# DAY 2: AFFIRMATIONS FOR SELF-BOUNDARIES

*"Love yourself enough to set boundaries. Your time and energy are precious and you get to decide how to use them. You teach people how to treat you by deciding what you will and won't accept." ~ Ann Taylor*

Being fully aware of yourself also means being fully aware of your boundaries. It is important to know your limits in terms of what you can and cannot give to preserve your sense of self. No one can take that away from you. No one.

To begin, take five deep breaths to center yourself. As you do so, pick a positive affirmation that resonates with you below and recite it to yourself ten times. It is best to do this in a quiet space or in front of a mirror. Take five more deep breaths when you are finished.

- *I am worthy and deserving of setting and maintaining boundaries that serve me.*
- *Each and every day, I'm becoming clearer and clearer about the boundaries that serve me best.*
- *It's easy for me to share my boundaries with others.*
- *It's safe for me to share my boundaries with others.*
- *I honor myself by honoring my boundaries.*
- *My boundaries help me take loving care of my body, mind, and soul each and every day, in each and every way.*
- *I easily attract ideal friends who honor and respect my boundaries.*
- *My boundaries help me grow as a person.*
- *I am ready to choose beautiful boundaries that help me live, create, and serve as the fullest expression of my incredible self.*
- *I now give myself permission to set boundaries that support my own self-worth.*

When you are ready, fill the following pages with your own affirmations for self-boundaries. Remember to be present, positive, and personal. After you recite your own affirmations, take five more deep breaths and give yourself a nice, big hug. Repeat this exercise as many times as you find helpful.

# DAY 3: AFFIRMATIONS FOR SELF-MINDSET

*"Believe you can, and you're halfway there."*
*~ Theodore Roosevelt*

Today is about cultivating an independent, growth mindset that attracts nothing but goodness and positivity into your lives. Trust your own instincts. It does not matter what other people think about you. You have the power, courage, and wisdom to be your own authentic self.

To begin, take five deep breaths to center yourself. As you do so, pick a positive affirmation that resonates with you below and recite it to yourself ten times. It is best to do this in a quiet space or in front of a mirror. Take five more deep breaths when you are finished.

- *I have the knowledge to make smart decisions for myself.*
- *I trust my intuition, and I always make wise decisions.*
- *As I take on new challenges, I feel calm, confident, and powerful.*
- *It does not matter what other people say or do. What matters is how I choose to react and what I choose to believe about myself.*
- *I am courageous. I am willing to act and face my fears.*
- *I have the power to create all the success and prosperity I desire.*
- *I am open-minded and always eager to explore new avenues to success.*
- *I choose to think positively and create a wonderful and successful life for myself.*
- *I am valuable and will make powerful contributions to the world today.*
- *Every challenge I face is an opportunity to grow and improve.*

When you are ready, fill the following pages with your own affirmations for self-mindset. Remember to be present, positive, and personal. After you recite your own affirmations, take five more deep breaths and give yourself a nice, big hug. Repeat this exercise as many times as you find helpful.

# DAY 4: AFFIRMATIONS FOR SELF-COMPASSION

*"This is a moment of suffering. Suffering is part of life. May I be kind to myself. May I give myself the compassion I need."*
*~Dr. Kristen Neff*

It may be easier for you to forgive others than yourself. Today, you will make space for self-compassion. We are all imperfect human beings, and it is important to cultivate loving kindness towards ourselves.

To begin, take five deep breaths to center yourself. As you do so, pick a positive affirmation that resonates with you below and recite it to yourself ten times. It is best to do this in a quiet space or in front of a mirror. Take five more deep breaths when you are finished.

- *I accept the best and worst parts of myself.*
- *Spending time with myself isn't selfish; it's essential.*
- *I am allowed to go easy on myself in times of stress.*
- *I am embracing myself just as I am.*
- *I am a work in progress, and that's okay.*
- *I accept my faults and quirks.*
- *I am allowed to be kind and gentle toward myself.*
- *I forgive myself for past mistakes and failures.*
- *I deserve to treat myself with the same compassion I give to others.*
- *I am choosing to love myself unconditionally.*

When you are ready, fill the following pages with your own affirmations for self-compassion. Remember to be present, positive, and personal. After you recite your own affirmations, take five more deep breaths and give yourself a nice, big hug. Repeat this exercise as many times as you find helpful.

# DAY 5: AFFIRMATIONS FOR SELF-RESILIENCE

*"Although the world is full of suffering, it is also full of the overcoming of it."*
*~ Helen Keller*

You have come quite the distance. Forgiving yourself through self-compassion is the start of cultivating self-resilience.

To begin, take five deep breaths to center yourself. As you do so, pick a positive affirmation that resonates with you below and recite it to yourself ten times. It is best to do this in a quiet space or in front of a mirror. Take five more deep breaths when you are finished.

- ○ *I have the power to pick myself up again.*
- ○ *I deserve the life I want.*
- ○ *I can rewrite my story.*
- ○ *I am bent, but not broken.*
- ○ *My faith has lifted me up before, and I can rely on it now.*
- ○ *My ability to conquer challenges is limitless, and my potential to succeed is infinite.*
- ○ *I know how to overcome the odds.*
- ○ *I allow doubt to float away from me.*
- ○ *I love how quickly I can adapt to change.*
- ○ *My scars are my armor.*

When you are ready, fill the following pages with your own affirmations for self-resilience. Remember to be present, positive, and personal. After you recite your own affirmations, take five more deep breaths and give yourself a nice, big hug. Repeat this exercise as many times as you find helpful.

# DAY 6: AFFIRMATIONS FOR SELF-HEALING

*"Healing is the end of conflict with yourself."*
*~ Stephanie Gailing*

Today can be tough for many of us, but part of learning to love yourself is learning to heal from trauma. It is about letting go of the past and living in the present moment. You deserve nothing but peace and serenity.

To begin, take five deep breaths to center yourself. As you do so, pick a positive affirmation that resonates with you below and recite it to yourself ten times. It is best to do this in a quiet space or in front of a mirror. Take five more deep breaths when you are finished.

- *I give myself permission to heal.*
- *I am willing to be at peace with myself and everyone.*
- *I release the past and trust that everything is happening for my greatest good.*
- *I bless the past and embrace the present moment with an open heart.*
- *I am determined to cure my wounds, soul, mind, and see things differently.*
- *I deserve peace to ensure my mental well-being.*
- *I do not hold a grudge against those who have hurt me. I prefer to be free and easy on myself.*
- *My hardships give me opportunities to promote myself.*
- *I am thriving in my healing journey.*
- *I release all emotional blocks that stop me from enjoying peace of mind.*

When you are ready, fill the following pages with your own affirmations for self-healing. Remember to be present, positive, and personal. After you recite your own affirmations, take five more deep breaths and give yourself a nice, big hug. Repeat this exercise as many times as you find helpful.

# DAY 7: AFFIRMATIONS FOR SELF-MOTIVATION

*"Push yourself, because no one else is going to do it for you."*
*~ Anonymous*

Today is about building self-motivation and confidence amidst adversity. You can accomplish anything and everything if you believe in yourself.

To begin, take five deep breaths to center yourself. As you do so, pick a positive affirmation that resonates with you below and recite it to yourself ten times. It is best to do this in a quiet space or in front of a mirror. Take five more deep breaths when you are finished.

- *I am stronger than I know.*
- *I am improving myself and getting closer to my goals every day.*
- *I will face the world with confidence.*
- *My body, mind, and spirit are powerful and profound.*
- *I have complete confidence in myself and my path.*
- *I know I can achieve anything I want in life.*
- *Today I am going to bid farewell to old bad habits and welcome a positive change in my life.*
- *I am the hero of my own life story.*
- *I am choosing to believe in myself today.*
- *I wake up today with strength in my heart and clarity in my mind.*

When you are ready, fill the following pages with your own affirmations for self-motivation. Remember to be present, positive, and personal. After you recite your own affirmations, take five more deep breaths and give yourself a nice, big hug. Repeat this exercise as many times as you find helpful.

# DAY 8: AFFIRMATIONS FOR SELF-GRATITUDE

*"Joy is the simplest form of gratitude."*
*~ Karl Barth*

You have healed from past traumas and picked yourself up with confidence in the past few days. Now is the time to reflect with gratitude for all of the goodness that has come into your life.

To begin, take five deep breaths to center yourself. As you do so, pick a positive affirmation that resonates with you below and recite it to yourself ten times. It is best to do this in a quiet space or in front of a mirror. Take five more deep breaths when you are finished.

- *I am eternally grateful for all of the blessings I have in my life.*
- *I am thankful that with each experience, I become a better version of myself.*
- *I live in a state of gratitude, and I am always thankful for the help and support of others who have helped me along the way.*
- *While I might not say it every day, I am always grateful for the love I receive. I try to give love to the best of my ability, and I am grateful for the love I have yet to receive.*
- *I wake up with a peaceful mind and a grateful heart.*
- *I exhale worry and inhale gratitude.*
- *I am grateful for the magic and miracles that today brings.*
- *I love and appreciate this moment in my life, exactly as it is right now.*
- *I am grateful for every step of this journey and the lessons I have learned along the way.*
- *I am grateful for myself.*

When you are ready, fill the following pages with your own self-gratitude affirmations. Remember to be present, positive, and personal. After you recite your own affirmations, take five more deep breaths and give yourself a nice, big hug. Repeat this exercise as many times as you find helpful.

# DAY 9: AFFIRMATIONS FOR SELF-ABUNDANCE

*"Abundance is not something we acquire; it is something we tune into."*
*~ Wayne Dyer*

Gratitude comes with an awareness of life's abundance and limitless possibilities. There may be days you feel drained and empty, but if you look deeply enough, there is life all around you. Embrace every moment of it.

To begin, take five deep breaths to center yourself. As you do so, pick a positive affirmation that resonates with you below and recite it to yourself at least ten times. It is best to do this in a quiet space or in front of a mirror. Take five more deep breaths when you are finished.

- *I have everything I need to be successful.*
- *I am open to limitless possibilities.*
- *I am grateful for the abundance that I have and the abundance that's on the way.*
- *I am surrounded by abundant love and laughter.*
- *My life is bursting with joy, love, and prosperity.*
- *My mind is free of limiting beliefs and open to the flow of everlasting abundance.*
- *I make space for love, abundance, and prosperity to flow to and through me.*
- *I live in a world filled with infinite love, and that love continually flows to and through me.*
- *I create ever-flowing abundance through joy, gratitude, and self-love.*
- *Everything I need to create infinite abundance is within me.*

When you are ready, fill the following pages with your own self-abundance affirmations. Remember to be present, positive, and personal. After you recite your own affirmations, take five more deep breaths and give yourself a nice, big hug. Repeat this exercise each and every day of this week.

# DAY 10: AFFIRMATIONS FOR SELF-LOVE

*"You yourself, as much as anybody in the entire universe, deserve your love and affection." ~ Buddha*

This is your last day on this *Be Your Own PAL* journey. Congratulations on a job well-done! We end this journey with the important theme of self-love. We need it more than ever. Learning to love yourself is one of the hardest things to do, but you can do it. You *can* love yourself truly, deeply, and unconditionally. In other words, you can be your own *PAL* if you believe it.

To begin, take five deep breaths to center yourself. As you do so, pick a positive affirmation that resonates with you below and recite it to yourself ten times. It is best to do this in a quiet space or in front of a mirror. Take five more deep breaths when you are finished.

- *I love myself just as I am today.*
- *I am amazing, inside and out.*
- *I am my own best friend.*
- *My body is healthy; my mind is brilliant; my soul is tranquil.*
- *I am grateful to be the person I am.*
- *I love each part of myself.*
- *I appreciate all the ways that I am unique.*
- *I love my perfectly imperfect self.*
- *I am beautiful, strong, and courageous.*
- *I am enough.*

When you are ready, fill the following page with your own self-love affirmations. Remember to be present, positive, and personal. After you recite your own affirmations, take five more deep breaths and give yourself a nice, big hug. Repeat this exercise as many times as you find helpful.

# BE YOU OWN PAL!

**CONGRATULATIONS ON FINISHING YOUR JOURNEY!**

**YOU ARE AMAZING.  KEEP SMILING AND BEING *YOU*.**

# ABOUT THE AUTHOR

**Duc Chung, MD, MBA, FAAHPM,** is a hospice and palliative care physician from Fresno, CA. He is a practicing Buddhist with a deep passion for mindfulness, meditation, and wellness. While faculty with the UCSF Fresno Hospice and Palliative Care Fellowship Program, he co-chaired the resiliency curriculum to help training physicians find peace, comfort, and healing in dealing with stressful patient encounters and life events. He is the recipient of many distinguished teaching awards and spreads his inspirations through his music website, www.ducchungmusic.com, or *Mind.Music.Medicine.* He is also the author of *Smile!,* a children's book to spread joy and positivity among children.

www.ingramcontent.com/pod-product-compliance
Lightning Source LLC
Chambersburg PA
CBHW050740150726

48196CB00003B/288